THE

25 Sales Habits

of *Highly Successful Salespeople*

by
Stephan Schiffman

ADAMS MEDIA CORPORATION
Avon, Massachusetts

Published by Adams Media, an F+W Publications Company
57 Littlefield Street, Avon, MA 02322 U.S.A.
www.adamsmedia.com

ISBN 13: 978-1-55850-391-5
ISBN 10: 1-55850-391-9

Printed in Canada.
T S R Q P O N

Library of Congress Cataloging-in-Publication Data

Schiffman, Stephan.
The 25 sales habits of highly successful salespeople / Stephan
Schiffman. – 2nd ed.
p.   m.
ISBN 1-55850-391-9
1. Selling. I. Title. II. Title: Twenty-five sales habits of highly
successful salespeople.
HF5438.25.S333   1994
659.85—dc20   94-15495
CIP

This publication is designed to provide accurate and authoritative information with regard to the subject matter covered. It is sold with the
understanding that the publisher is not engaged in rendering legal,
accounting, or other professional advice. If legal advice or other expert
assistance is required, the services of a competent professional person
should be sought.
— From a *Declaration of Principles* jointly adopted by a Committee of the
American Bar Association and a Committee of Publishers and Associations

This book is available at quantity discounts for bulk purchases.
For information, call 1-800-289-0963

To your future

Also by Stephan Schiffman:

*The 25 Most Common Sales Mistakes
and How to Avoid Them*

*The 25 Most Dangerous Sales Myths
and How to Avoid Them*

*The 25 Sales Habits of Highly
Successful Salespeople*

*The 25 Sales Skills They Don't Teach
at Business School*

*The 25 Sales Strategies That Will Boost
Your Sales Today!*

The 250 Sales Questions to Close the Deal

Ask Questions, Get Sales

Beat Sales Burnout

*Closing Techniques (That Really Work!),
3rd Edition*

*Cold Calling Techniques (That Really Work!),
5th Edition*

Power Sales Presentations

Stephan Schiffman's Telesales

Upselling Techniques (That Really Work!)

Contents

Acknowledgments

I would like to thank the following people for their help with this book: my editor Brandon Toropov; Michele Reisner, for her aid in developing the original concept; Lynne Einleger for her encouragement; and, of course, Anne, Daniele, and Jennifer for their unceasing support.

Introduction

How has the sales landscape changed over the past ten or fifteen years?

That question occurred to me while I was working with a sales manager at a *Fortune* 500 firm who complained that his salespeople "still thought it was the early eighties."

The more I thought about his (accurate) observation, the more I was reminded that these habits, first outlined in book form three years ago, really do highlight the strategies used nowadays by successful salespeople—the ones who have adapted to all the changes in today's competitive selling environment. And since then, my work with salespeople has convinced me of the point. This new edition—revised to include some additional insights on a number of key points—reflects an opportunity for you to benefit from these habits for success by incorporating them into your sales routine. (And, yes, you can add a good habit to your routine—just as you can add a bad one!)

■　　■　　■

For my money, selling is the most exciting job in the world. With the right organization, it gives you unlimited income potential, freedom, and a clear means to take control of your career and your life. I believe it beats any other occupation hands down. But there's a problem.

In the seminars that my company conducts, the first question we ask of salespeople is, "What's the one thing you would like to change about your job?" The answer we get is always the same: "The attitude people have toward what we do for a living!"

Often, people simply doesn't trust salespeople. Part of that has to do with personal contact with flim-flam artists. Part of it has to do with media images of salespeople. Whether it's a crazy used car salesman in an obnoxious commercial or a shifty, fast-talking wheeler-dealer on some crime drama, salespeople *never* seem to come off in the media as hard-working, concerned, accountable professionals. The negative stereotypes are reinforced thousands of times a day.

Of course, there really are people out there who look for a quick buck, shout a lot, and keep an eye open for new office space when customers have problems. But this book won't help them. This book is for us. The good guys. The salespeople who want to build business relationships, deliver results, and stand behind what's delivered. But when we knock on the door, who does our prospect think of? Those thousand yellow-jacketed pitchmen who talk too fast and don't care in the least about the prospect's viewpoint, that's who! Sometimes we lose sales—not because of what we've done, but because of what the people who have come before us have done.

This book will help you demonstrate the poise, professionalism, and accountability that is *required* of today's successful salesperson. This book will show you twenty-five traits that will help you instantly distinguish yourself from the amateurs your prospect may be confusing you with. This book is your blueprint for achievement in the fastest-paced, most dynamic profession in business.

■　　■　　■

Earlier, I pointed out that a lot has changed in business—and in sales—since the late seventies and early eighties. Before we move on to the habits for success, let's review three of the most important points today's salesperson must bear in mind.

First and most important, you must remember that your prospects are more value-conscious and *information-conscious* than ever. From the first instant of your contact with a new sales prospect, you must be prepared to demonstrate your patterns of success with previous customers, and you had better be able to discuss, chapter and verse, the specific benefits you've delivered. Similarly, you must also bring to your first meeting with the prospect a recognizable expertise in your business area. That doesn't mean you need to memorize the encyclopedia before you close a sale, and it certainly doesn't mean that you should throw around a lot of fancy language the prospect won't understand. But in this time-pressed, data-sensitive age of ours, you must demonstrate to the prospect that your organization brings a unique and impressive knowledge and skill base to its business relationships.

Secondly (and this comes as a surprise to many salespeople), you must take an aggressive presentation stance that does *not* necessarily focus on the prospect's own perceived "needs." For decades, we were told to focus exclusively on these self-defined "needs" of the prospect, but a more accurate way to state the matter now would be to say that you are responsible for helping to define the requirements. With staffs stretched to the breaking point and managers juggling fifteen different balls at once, your prospect may not even *know* about an impending problem or lost opportunity! These days, when you "need" something, it's usually because the president of your company has told you to attend to a particular problem—and believe me, in those circumstances, you don't wait around for a salesperson to give you a call. You head out to the widget factory and set it up yourself. So don't focus so much on "needs." The key to selling in today's fast-paced environment is to ask people what they do, how they do it, when and where they do it, why they do it that way, and how you can help them do it better. The successful salesperson today is more attuned to the "do" than to the "need."

Finally, today's successful salesperson is *willing to think ahead*. That means consistently looking for the next step in the sales process. That means prospecting for tomorrow—and maintaining a prospect base, even if you're given an existing account base to work with. That means anticipating common objections and avoiding unproductive exchanges with prospects. And that means being willing to change approaches that aren't working now, even if they worked in the past. In the final analysis, thinking ahead means taking responsibility for your own career. For the real salesperson, the person who loves a challenge and loves to be in the driver's seat, that's no problem at all.

■   ■   ■

Make no mistake. You're going to have to fight to win and keep customers. Intense competition is a fact of life in today's market. The time for complacency in sales, if there ever was one, is long past.

There are a lot of salespeople out there today competing for the business you work hard to obtain. Some of them do a very good job, make a lot of money, and stick around, building satisfying careers that last for decades. Others try to wing it and burn out. I've worked with both kinds. The habits that distinguish the former from the latter are in this book. They can work for you.

Good luck!

— *Stephan Schiffman*
New York, New York

Habit #1

Communicating the message that it is sound business to trust you

I've trained over a quarter of a million salespeople. And the more salespeople I run into, the more exposure I get to various "tricks of the trade"—little corners salespeople cut in order to get ahead (or so they think) over the short term. The only problem is, too many of these "tricks of the trade" undercut an essential objective: that of constantly sending and reinforcing the message that it is a good business decision to trust you.

The "raffle" and its consequences when it comes to building long-term partnerships

I know a car dealer who uses such a "trick" to get people to come into his showroom. He opens up the white pages, finds a name, calls the person, and says, "Hi, Mr. Jones, this is Mike Johnson at Johnson Used Cars. You've just won our raffle! Come on in and collect a turkey!" What he never says is that he really wants the person to come in and collect two turkeys: one to put in the oven, and the other for the driveway. (By the way, there is no raffle; the turkeys are bought as premiums for anyone who walks through the door.)

The same salesperson would call up someone at random and claim to have found his wallet, "just to get his attention," then launch into his pitch. How much would you trust an approach like that?

I'm not trying to be harsh toward those who sell automobiles for a living. Some of the most effective salespeople I know sell used cars. But I am trying to say something about this used car salesman. By starting off with "Hey, you've won a free turkey," he was using a cheap trick. It seems to me that it was no coincidence that he sold cars to match. Word gets around about that sort of thing.

If you sell turkeys, talk about turkeys. If you sell cars, talk about cars. Talk about exactly why it makes perfect sense to buy the one you have to offer. Beware of the "tricks of the trade." If they come at the expense of your credibility, they're too expensive.

"Follow me!"

The successful salesperson makes a *good leader* because he or she inspires trust. I think that the truly successful salespeople today—and, by the way, this is what I see in world-class sales forces—have the personal magnetism and the self-assurance to say to people, "Follow me"—and thereby win long-term, happy customers. That kind of authority only comes with complete, unflinching confidence that you can deliver results for your prospect. If you're right, your customers trust you—and follow you.

Building trustworthiness, then, means *building leadership skills*. That's not to say you should practice railroading your customers! All the confidence and authority in the world won't change the "I-found-that-wallet-you-never-really-lost" scam into a way to build trust. It means understanding your product or service, understanding what your prospects do for a living, and assuming responsibility for delivering results to your customers, no matter what. Prospects can sense when this is what you're offering, and they like it.

What makes a good leader?

- A good leader has a vision.
- A good leader commands respect.
- A good leader sees the big picture.
- A good leader knows when to change direction.

- A good leader points out problem areas and is ready to discuss solutions.

- A good leader has confidence in both approach and attitude.

- And a good leader is accountable.

All of these traits add up to true trustworthiness.

The real thing

Too many salespeople focus on whether or not they have learned to *appear* trustworthy. That's not the point! You want to develop an earned reputation for following through on everything—and I mean every syllable—that comes out of your mouth. That means, for one thing, absolute punctuality. If you say you'll call at 9:00 A.M., then call at 9:00 A.M., and not 9:02 A.M. Better yet, call at 8:55 A.M. and be willing to be put on hold! Some salespeople take this principle and turn it into a recipe for annoyance; others display the spark of professionalism necessary to demonstrate dependability and consistence as personal hallmarks.

If you think such "minor details" don't have any real persuasive power, I have to disagree with you. At the beginning of your relationship with a prospect, those "details" are all he or she has to go on. They're the only tool you have! Spout lavish promises, and fail to follow through on the "details," and you'll be like every other salesperson. But say you're ready, within the next five minutes, to fax over a quote that completely meets all the prospect's specifications, then *do it* . . . and you're one in a million.

Relationships are built on trust, and trust is built on evidence of all kinds. This does not mean that you must show that you're subservient—that's the opposite of being a leader! You must demonstrate that you are unfailingly dependable in all things, big and small, and you must make a habit of delivering what you promised (or, preferably, more). Then you will be in a position to say with authority, "Follow me."

Habit #2

Asking the right questions

Ask important questions. Ask real questions. If you need to rely on "How's the weather?" or "Have a nice weekend?" for your opening, fine. But thereafter, base everything you ask on a simple principle: never waste the prospect's time. That may seem like an obvious point, but it certainly isn't treated like one by most sales-people! Know when it's time to move beyond the litany of pointless observations on decor, golf, the weather, or whatever. You came here on a business appointment. There will come a point at which your client will be ready to move past the small talk. Do so, tactfully.

A single question to help you make the transition into the "Business End" of the conversation

How do you start asking the important questions? I'm going to suggest that you start with a simple one—a question that may seem to have nothing to do with your visit, but that will actually yield some remarkable insights into the kind of person you're working with.

"Just out of curiosity, Ms. Allen—how did you get this job?"

That will ease you into the "business end" of the visit quite nicely, and will also encourage your contact to open up to you. After your prospect has had the chance to answer in whatever degree of detail he or she feels comfortable with, you might continue by saying what you have in mind—why you're talking to the person in the first place—and explaining why you're going over this (so your later questions will make more sense).

"Ms. Allen, we handle the top-selling line of widgets in the United States of America. Let me tell you a little bit about how we work. My only job during this first meeting is to find out about your business; I didn't come here to sell anything today. I mention that because I wanted to ask you a few questions about your store, to find out if I really can help you boost your sales volume. Have you got a moment for that?"

What do you do once you've told the prospect a (very) little about your business solutions?

Assuming you get a "yes" to the question that ends that little speech (and that's a pretty good bet), you can then move on to the big questions.

(Question One—The Past:) "Have you ever used any of our widgets before?" ("If so, how did they work out?")

(Question Two—The Present:) "Just out of curiosity, what widget are you presently using?" ("How do you feel about it?")

(Question Three—The Future:) "Tell me something; what do the next six months look like for you in terms of widget use?" ("How do you plan to use widgets to reach goal X?")

If you feel uncomfortable moving into "serious" areas, like whether or not the firm uses or might use your products, but you still feel certain that you have passed the point at which you can discuss last night's baseball game, there are a number of middle-ground questions you can pose before getting to the heart of the matter. Here are some suggestions.

- "Tell me, what kind of customers do you serve?"

- "What other locations do you have?" (Or: "Where are your headquarters located?")

- "What kind of sales force do you use?"

- "How long has the firm been in business?"
- "What kinds of challenges do you face in this business/industry?"

Such questions may well yield important information for you, and can serve as an effective "bridge" to the main point of your visit. But beware of overreliance on such middle-ground questions; my guess is that your contact is, like most of us these days, short on time. Most prospects will appreciate your getting to the point in short order, and you can do this without jeopardizing the emerging relationship.

The last "right question"

The last "right question" of your first visit usually sounds something like this:

"You know, Mr. Jones, I've learned a lot today, and I want to thank you for taking the opportunity to talk to me. Let me tell you what I usually do at this stage. I think we're at that point now where I need to set up another appointment for us, one where I can come back after having sorted through everything I've learned here, and show you what we may be able to do for your company. Is Tuesday at three okay?"

Habit #3

Taking the lead

Tell the prospect where you are at any given point in the sales cycle. Don't be afraid to steer the conversation in the direction you want it to go.

Here's what it might sound like

"Mr. Prospect, I want to thank you very much for taking time out to see me today. I know we have a lot to go over, but during this part of the visit what I usually do is give some information about my company and what we do. We've been in business since . . . ."

"Mr. Prospect, at this stage I'd like to ask a couple of simple questions that will help me find out ways we can help you."

"Well, now that we've come this far, Mr. Prospect,

I'll tell you what I'd like to do. I'd like to take these notes and go back to my office and see if we can work up a proposal for you, then meet again next week. Would Friday at two be okay?"

"Certainly good to meet with you again, Mr. Prospect. Now that we've worked up this proposal, I think it would be a good idea for me to take a few minutes to just summarize it for you here, and then answer any questions you may have."

"So that's our proposal, Mr. Prospect. I have a feeling we will really be able to put this program into place for you successfully. At this point in the process, my feeling is that the sooner we get this underway, the better it will be for your company. Is Saturday the twelfth of December a good day to start?"

The perils of doing anything and everything to avoid offending the prospect

How many presentations are sabotaged by salespeople who want to avoid "offending"—and never get around to mentioning the reason they stepped in the door in the first place? Take charge. Make a conscious choice to inform the prospect with regard to where you both are in the process. The alternative is long, "good" meetings that end in that odd, result-free limbo that leaves neither party sure what to do next.

We don't live in a perfect world. We live in a world of complex people who have complex thinking patterns— people whose next action may not be obvious to us. It follows, then, that we run the risk of having the prospect stop us and say, "Hold on—wait a minute. I'm not ready for that yet. You're moving too fast for me."

So what?

You need that information. You need to know where there is still a problem to be worked on. If you don't know where there's a problem, you won't be able to close the sale. And it's far better to isolate a problem through a consistent system of "sequence updates" (as I like to call them) than to wait until the last minute, ask for the business, and then find out there was something important you should have been paying attention to but weren't.

Getting the information you'll need to move ahead in the sales cycle—even if it's not what you want to hear

Sometimes, as a result of these updates and the feedback you receive from then, you will isolate issues the prospect has not yet brought to the surface. You may find that, even though you went in the door thinking about selling Widget A, and even though the prospect seems interested enough in Widget A, the questions that keep coming up as you try to move the process along seem to concern the applications you know can only be obtained through Widget B! Your objective is to solve problems—not to make the prospect fit your preconceptions! So you move on to Widget B. But you can only do this because you've listened to the feedback your updates have yielded.

Let's be clear on one thing: sales cycles will vary from industry to industry and from customer to customer. What that means in plain English is that you never know when someone's going to agree to buy something. I'm not suggesting that you try to manhandle the prospect. Even if you issue the updates I'm talking about, you still have to be willing to work with the prospect, every step of the way. The key point is, you can't do that unless you both know where you are—and where you're going.

Habit #4

Engaging the prospect

Engaging the prospect is a subtle undertaking; it is difficult to define. I should start out by telling you what it's
not. Engaging the prospect is not reacting instantane-
ously, as if by reflex, to every comment or perceived
disapproval. Consider this exchange.

Prospect: The last time we worked in this area, I'll
never forget, the first session was on a Monday morning, and . . . .

You: Oh, well, we can work on Mondays. Mondays are no problem.

Prospect: Well, actually, what I was going to say was
that since it was a Monday morning, we
didn't have quite the eager spirit that we

might have preferred . . .

You: I see, I see. Well, we can do it on any day you want.

That's not engaging anyone. That's ping-pong. Engaging your prospect means going beyond slapshot, automatic exchanges. It requires that you so clearly respond to stated or unstated requirements (not all of which will have to do with your product or service), that you establish a core of understanding and a framework within which both you and your prospect can solve important problems. You will have to find, for yourself, the best way to establish that connection, given the particular dynamics of a given prospect's age, position, gender, or even race, in comparison with yours. It is pointless to ignore such differences among people, and virtually suicidal not to accommodate them in a sales setting.

Your prospect's unique circumstances

Every prospect is different. Every prospect reacts differently to what you have to say. Some seem to have all the time in the world, others consider a fifteen-minute meeting to be a major crisis in time management. Some have made careers out of being skeptical, others pride themselves on freethinking, even outrageous approaches to problems. The point is, you cannot earn the respect of all of them with a single "script" designed to "handle the first few minutes." You must identify what is important to any given prospect, then learn how to appeal to those values.

Here are some general suggestions on drawing out your prospect and initiating meaningful initial conversations. Of course, you will have to adapt them to fit particular situations.

Discuss that with which you are comfortable and familiar. Avoid venturing opinions on Abstract Expressionism if you know nothing about that branch of modern art; do offer your insights on model trains, Disney collectibles, or memory improvements if the topic in question is one you have an informed interest in. Your confidence in the subject you select—and connect somehow to your prospect—will carry over. (Note: There is an advantage to beginning an exchange by focusing on your own observations and experiences—adroitly and tactfully, of course. Doing so takes some of the pressure off of your prospect, who will be expecting you to try to "draw him in.")

Discuss the surroundings. The office you will be sitting in is a reflection of its occupant. Surely you can find, with little difficulty, something that will serve as a positive conversational starting point that has to do with the way your prospect has chosen to decorate his or her surroundings.

Support the prospect in subtle ways

When the person starts to talk about himself, "lean in"

to the conversation. I also put down the pen I'm using to take notes. This serves as a subtle validation that the prospect's experiences are inherently interesting. (It is virtually always good to get the prospect discussing his or her own experiences. People who talk about themselves are more relaxed than people who don't.)

Show care by really caring. Remember, you're there to help. When the prospect outlines a problem, show the same concern you would if it were yours. (After all, you want it be yours!)

Habit #5

Finding key requirements

Should you set your goal as that of "finding customers who need the product?" All the time? The answer is more complicated than you might think.

News flash: the economy has changed—and you should, too, if you want to succeed

Most of us who are selling today are not creating a new market. That is to say, we're not following the time-honored advice to "find a need and fill it," because, on the whole, we can't. Our economy has been eradicating basic needs on an historically unprecedented scale for almost a half-century now, and it's done a pretty darned good job. Not a perfect job, of course, but a good enough job to change the way most salespeople must operate. What 'oday's salespeople must do to succeed is find requirements they can fill among those sought-after, qualified buyers who know full well that the choice is theirs when it comes to choosing the new widget service.

We have a lot of automobiles in this country. We have a lot of copiers. And we have a whole bunch of health care plans available, too. If it is your job to sell an automobile, a copier, or a health care plan, you will have to come up with something new and exciting about your particular offer for a given buyer who, these days, can more and more be counted on to have some experience with your product or service category. You will have to tailor your approach to the requirements you are identifying within such prospect groups. Otherwise, you will have some problems.

Find the prospect who fits your profile of a happy customer, and work from there

This is not to say that there is no such thing as a first-time car buyer, or a company that is shopping around for its first health plan. Obviously, the patterns of "new" buyers will vary from region to region and from industry to industry. My point is, most good salespeople I meet do not make "virgin" prospects their core concern. Their objective, typically, is not to identify a need for the widget, but to get a lead on the type of widget buyer/user whose requirements they can satisfy better than anyone else—then make some striking comparisons to that person.

Find your segment, your area of expertise, your niche. Learn to classify common concerns and problems shared by the types of "educated" customers you know you have been able to satisfy. Then prospect for that person. Of course, you aren't going to turn anyone down who doesn't fit your profile and still wants to buy from you. But most successful salespeople I know develop a sense of who the likely customer is—and then put themselves in front of as many of those types of people as possible.

With someone who's been using Brand X widgets for twenty years, your goal will not be identifying the need—it will be unearthing the requirements that will have to be met before your prospect will consider changing to your Brand Y widgets.

Does he require a better service plan? More flexibility with payments? A better price? Frequent contact with you the salesperson? There are a million variations. Often the requirements will be difficult to gauge; perhaps the prospect himself has not fully identified them. That's where you come in.

The salesperson as tactful educator and facilitator—not steamroller

Of course, there are some fields of sales in which the primary focus may well be on first-time buyers; insurance comes to mind. Here, too, however, it is a little simplistic to look at the process as simply "finding a need." Any good insurance agent can tell you that a major part of his job is educating—filling in the knowledge gaps the first-time buyer brings to the table, and then providing the information necessary for that person to make the right choice. This requires no small degree of tact, patience, and persistence—all for a considerable period of time after the need is found.

Think about it. If you're a person who "needs" life insurance, and who does not require any assistance or new information to get to that point, what are you going to do? Call up the life insurance company!

Remember: In dealing with a customer who already uses a competing product or service—as we so often must—we have to remember that the need itself has already been established. It has been so firmly established that the person has opted to take time out of a very busy schedule to meet with you and discuss it. More sales than you might imagine have been lost because of a salesperson's inability to grasp that the focus with the "educated" customer must be on how to identify and meet new requirements that the current product or service is not meeting.

The importance of perspective—and patience—in dealing with your prospects

Keep things in perspective here. No one is suggesting you should not talk up your products—and vigorously!

It's all a question of how. Prattling on about how wonderful Brand Y widgets are, when compared to no widgets, is suicidal. Discussing the specific ways Brand Y widgets will deliver more, perform better, or make for a more attractive budget than Brand X is the way you will make the sale.

Look at each lead as a sales relationship—and remember that relationships take time to develop.

Habit #6

Converting the leads that "fall into your lap"

It's a dream come true.

You're on the job, minding your own business, when suddenly someone calls, seemingly out of the blue, and virtually asks you for business. Wow!

I know what the first temptation is. You want to close the sale. Life is tough enough; you spend all day building, establishing, persuading. Now along comes The Sale You Deserve, and you're sure as heck not going to let it slip through your fingers. So you start to move in.

Don't.

It will take some discipline. (Let's be honest; it will

take a lot of discipline.) But if you really want to move the lead from the other end of the receiver onto your commission check, I promise you that the surest way to do it is to take a deep breath, count three, and follow a few simple steps.

Three steps to follow

One: Back off and establish some kind of relationship. If this really is someone you've never spoken to before, you don't know whether or not a brusque, let's-get-right-down-to-business, well-of-course-we-can-solve-your-problem approach is going to work. It may backfire spectacularly, and often has. So exchange a few pleasantries; get a feeling for the kind of person you're talking to.

Two: Find out what's going on. Say, "I'm really glad you got in touch with me; listen, do you mind if I ask what prompted your call?" This is very important! You have to know exactly what you're dealing with; no sale exists in a vacuum. Things may not be what they seem! Sometimes people call, sound like they're going to sign on, but really need generous amounts of tender loving care. Establish your surroundings; get the information. Don't succumb to the temptation to sell—it may be too early.

Three: Ask to set up an in-person appointment. Yes, even if the person tries to close the sale himself on the phone. (Unless, of course, you're involved with telemarketing.) You need to establish a personal bond.

Don't assume you've got a "sure thing." Sales is a numbers game; your objective is to turn the odds in your favor in as many different ways, and on as many different occasions, as humanly possible.

If you do that over the long haul, it will pay off handsomely.

Habit #7

Knowing how to make your product or service fit somewhere else

How can you adapt an existing product or service to satisfy a prospect?

In my seminars, I talk a lot about product/service "malleability"; the word means "flexibility" or "capacity of being adapted."

Dentists use gold and silver for fillings because of the malleability of those metals; they are easily manipulated, and provide a complete, secure fit over and within a cavity. Along the same lines, you might want to think about the ways your product or service can be adjusted or customized for new prospects to meet specific requirements.

The paper clip

Let's take a look at a simple example. Suppose you're in the paper clip business. How many ways do you think you could use paper clips? Obviously, you can think of a paper clip as a small metal item used to fasten sheets of paper together. But if you stop and think about it for a moment, you'll realize that people use paper clips for all kinds of different purposes. Some people twist them into makeshift cotter pins; some people use them to clean out hard-to-reach places on office equipment; some people use them to fix eyeglasses; some people make decorative chains out of them. I personally have used (with great care!) two paper clips as a tiny clamp to extract a stubborn disk that would not eject from my computer's drive.

There are probably a hundred different uses for a paper clip besides holding sheets of paper together. Are there a hundred different uses for your product or service that you may not have considered before? Before you dismiss this possibility, keep in mind that you don't need a hundred to boost your sales. You just need one.

Baking soda is for cooking, right? Well, it can be . . . but for some strange reason the Arm and Hammer people insist on running these ads promoting its use as a refrigerator deodorizer. By the way, do you know anyone who uses baking soda that way now?

We all know you're not supposed to play with your food. Or are you? The people who make Jell-O think you should. They launched a huge media campaign that was intended solely to familiarize consumers with the idea of making Jigglers cookie cutter shapes out of gelatin, then letting the kids play with the Jell-O before devouring it. They gave away the Jiggler molds for free with any Jell-O purchase. An informal study of the market results (i.e., me watching what the people in front of me in line have brought to the checkout counter) yields the admittedly unscientific observation that a heck of a lot more people than usual seem to be buying Jell-O—and buying it six, eight, or even twelve packs at a time.

That's product malleability.

Ask yourself!

Does what you sell work in only one way? Or can you adjust it? Can you make it serve some new purpose or function? Can you present it in a different light, or to a different group of people? The key lies in opening your own mind to new possibilities, then following through.

This is not to say that you have to become another Henry Ford or Thomas Edison to make this principle work for you. Keep it simple to begin with. You can start with just one variation. If it's a winner, you may very well find that it can change not only your career in sales, but perhaps also change the business you work for!

Habit #8

Pretending you're a consultant (because you are)

Treat all your sales work as a consulting assignment.

Many years ago, I found myself hopelessly stuck while working with a new prospect. I was trying to develop a program for him, and things simply weren't working out.

So here's what I did. I said, "Charlie, rather than go any further with this, let me think about what we've talked about here and come back next week with a couple of ideas. Then, if you like them, we can continue our discussion." He agreed to that; I eventually closed the sale.

It was shortly after that meeting that I realized what I had done. I had taken the same approach I would normally take with a client who was simply asking for an evaluation of the problems on his firm's sales staff. I had taken the "sell" sign down for a moment and come to grips with the fact that, since I did not yet have an adequate assessment of the prospect's problems, I could not offer him a solution.

There's a catch to selling from the mindset of the consultant. You have to be willing to stop and think once in a while.

Solving problems

The best salespeople are professional problem solvers. If you sell cars, then you should consider yourself in the business of solving transportation problems. If you sell copiers, then you should consider yourself in the business of solving photocopying problems. If you sell cellular phones, then you should consider yourself in the business of solving communication problems. But you have to know and understand the problem first, before you can try to solve it. You have to be willing to walk in the door without any preconceived notions as to how best to solve the problems identified.

For many salespeople, the consulting principle can be put on an even simpler footing. If you sell to other companies, you should consider yourself in the business of solving profitability problems. That's the key concern you will ultimately be addressing: how to increase profitability. Everything you do, every proposal you offer, should lead eventually to the goal of your client's firm increasing its level of profitability. Weight your goals and your approaches against this standard, and you will have gone a long way toward achieving sales success.

If you're not interested in helping people solve problems, then I'm going to respectfully suggest that you're not in the right business. If you can't break everything you do down into something that helps another person reach an important goal, you will either base your sales on manipulating others or fail to persuade prospects that you are offering anything of value. Either path leads inexorably to burnout and/or constant rejection. You definitely don't need that.

You could look it up

The dictionary defines "consult" as "to seek advice, information, or guidance from." To me, this definition encapsulates exactly the relationship between a qualified prospect and a professional salesperson. You as a salesperson are there to advise the prospect as to the ways you can help solve existing problems; to provide all necessary information relative to solving those problems; and to provide the necessary guidance that will result in a harmonious professional association.

Act like a consultant . . . because that's really what you are!

Habit #9

Asking for the next appointment while you're on the first visit

This is perhaps the easiest piece of advice to follow in this book. Yet it is also a step that salespeople routinely ignore. Many are even *afraid* to take it even though they know it has done wonders for others!

A young salesperson once actually said to me, "Steve, that's not my place. I'm in the prospect's office. He's showing me a courtesy by seeing me in the first place. If I'm going to go back there for a second visit, the prospect should ask me."

Baloney!

You initiated the contact in the first place. You have made it clear at every point in the process that your objective is to help the prospect. You have demonstrated that you are interested primarily in solving a problem for him. Why on earth shouldn't you ask the prospect for the next appointment so you can show how you would implement the solution?

Excuses, excuses

This point is—to me, at any rate—so basic that it requires little argument in its favor. Yet it never ceases to amaze me how much bewildered amazement greets me when I suggest it to salespeople. Here are some actual answers I've received from salespeople in response to the suggestion that they set up their next appointment during the first visit.

"I can't ask for the appointment; I don't know when I'll be back in the area."

"I can't ask for the appointment; I don't know how long it will take me to write the proposal."

"I can't ask for the appointment; I don't have a quote ready for the prospect yet."

"I can't ask for the appointment; he may not want to give it to me."

These are real, honest-to-goodness salespeople talking! Can you believe it?

If you have to make rough guesses at the amount of time it will take you to pull a quote together or coordinate with one of your team members, then guess!

What's the worst that could happen. You call up the prospect's office to reschedule. Big deal.

Your objective

You didn't set the initial appointment for your health. You did it because you had an objective: helping to solve the prospect's problem with your product or service. You still have that objective at the conclusion of your initial visit; therefore, it is altogether appropriate for you to ask to move the process along to the next stage before the meeting adjourns.

Unless you receive a firm, unequivocal "no" at the first meeting, there will always be a next stage to talk about. And the best possible time to set the appointment for discussing that next stage is right then. You both have your calendars within reach. You both have pens or pencils handy. What other time would you choose to set your next meeting? What on earth would induce you to leave that room without knowing when you will next meet with the person?

> "Okay, Mr. Jones; I think we've gone about as far with this as we can today. What I'd like to do is meet with you a couple of weeks from now to show you exactly what we can do for your company. How's Friday the fifteenth?"

Listen for the response. (There has to be a response of some kind!) Then work from there with the information you receive.

Habit #10

Taking notes

Taking notes during your meeting with the prospect can be one of your most powerful sales tools.

Focusing on solutions

Taking notes will reinforce, both for you and the prospect, the reason you showed up in the first place: to learn more about the prospect's problem.

Listening

Taking notes helps you listen. There's something about having an empty sheet of paper in front of you that really tunes you in to what is being said, and makes it more difficult for you to miss important points.

Authority

Taking notes puts you in a position of authority and control. Believe me, during the opening twenty minutes or so of most first-time sales visits, you can use all the help here you can get.

Analytical abilities

Taking notes strengthens your analytical abilities. If you write down notes during your interview, you're using three senses: touch (that is, your hand, which is doing the writing), hearing (what you have to do to listen to the prospect) and sight (to see what you've written). My experience has been that by approaching a problem through tactile, visual, and aural stimuli, you're usually in a much better position to come up with a solution.

Getting the prospect to share information

Taking notes will encourage the prospect to open up. You may doubt this, but don't knock it until you've tried it. Every time I conduct a seminar, I get further proof of how effective the simple act of writing something down (in this case, on an easel) can be in encouraging communication. When I simply stand in front of an audience and ask, "What was good about the presentation we just heard?"—nothing happens. When I stand in front of an easel and write "GOOD POINTS IN PRESENTATION" across the top, then ask for suggestions—wham! The room comes alive!

Positive signals

Taking notes sends strong positive signals to the prospect, and you can never do that too much. When the prospect says, I have 500 trucks, each of which holds 75 widgets, making deliveries 320 days a year," and then looks over and sees that you've written "500 x 75 widgets x 320 days/yr," guess what? You've scored! You care! You're listening!

Some suggestions

I'd suggest you use a standard yellow pad with a hard cardboard backing. It needs to be stiff enough for you to be able to write while it's on your lap. Keep your notes clean and spare; remember that they should be legible to both you and the prospect at all times. Where appropriate, draw oversized diagrams in your notes to emphasize a point you're making verbally—and show your diagrams to the prospect.

Habit #11

Creating a plan with each new prospect

I go through a little monologue each time I meet a new prospect. I say, "Here's someone new. Here's someone I've never met before. What am I going to do that will be a little different with this person?"

It may be routine for you, but the prospect you're dealing with has never gone through the sales cycle with you before. One of the best ways I know of to combat that "here I go again" sensation (and that's a danger for even the very best salespeople) is to produce a customized, written plan for your prospect. This should be based on the material you gather in your notes during the first and subsequent meetings.

"Oh, *that* again."

After a while, you become familiar with certain objections or problems. And it's all too easy to pigeonhole your prospect. "I know that one; that's just like the problem the guy at ABC Company had." Well, it is and it isn't. It is not like the ABC problem in that the person who just outlined it has nothing to do with ABC Company, and probably faces a number of different challenges related to the problem he just brought up.

A prospect who offers up an objection is really making a gesture of good faith. That may sound a little bizarre, but it's true. By taking the time to share a concern or problem with you, your prospect is passing along important information, key facts on the way your product or service needs to be adapted. Listening is the first part of the secret, and identifying the mutually accepted solutions is the second part.

Find out what those challenges are, being sure to be aware of the unique circumstances or background your prospect may face. Then commit the solutions to paper, working with your prospect to determine the outline of the plan that will make the most sense in the current situation.

Doctor, doctor . . .

If you go to the doctor because you have a stomach ache, you don't care if he's seen three thousand other people with stomach aches over the course of his long and illustrious career. The last thing you want is for him to rush in the room, look you up and down, mumble some technical phrase you've never heard before, and scratch something on a prescription pad before hustling away again.

No. You want him to ask how you feel, how long you've felt that way, whether you've ever felt that way before, exactly where it hurts, what medicines you may be allergic to, and any other pertinent questions. If a doctor does all that, you're likely to be a better patient- and you'll probably have a better attitude about coming to see him next time.

You're a doctor. It doesn't matter how many patients you've seen before. This one is the only one you're seeing now. Like the best doctors, you should make an effort to include the patient in your diagnosis and treatment. Doing so not only makes for a better atmosphere for you to conduct your work in, it also increases the likelihood that your patient will have the positive attitude that is really the driving force behind so many dramatic recoveries!

Habit #12

Asking for referrals

My favorite story about referrals has to do with a very successful salesperson I know named Bill. Every year he vacations in some exotic locale like Fiji or the Cayman Islands or Hawaii. Often, these vacations come as a result of company bonuses for his performance or industry awards. So about once a year, this agent sends a letter to his customers and qualified prospects announcing his return from Paradise, where he received the XYZ Award for Outstanding Salesmanship. The purpose of the letter is to thank the salesperson's clients for their business, and to make it perfectly clear that the only way the salesperson has been able to attain his goals is by helping customers attain theirs. Classy, yes?

At the end of the letter is a paragraph that runs

something like this: "As you know, my business depends upon referrals. I would very much appreciate if you would take a moment now to jot down the names and phone numbers of three or four people in the industry you feel might benefit from talking to me. Of course, if you do not wish me to use your name when contacting these people, all you have to do is indicate this in the space I've provided below. Again, thank you for your business, and here's to continuing success for both of us."

Call me crazy. But I have a feeling there may be some cause-and-effect connection between letters like that and all those expensive vacations and impressive sales awards.

The numbers speak

Let's play a little multiplication game. Suppose five people give you five referrals each, for a total of twenty-five. And suppose that, of those new referrals, sixty percent turn around and give you five referrals, too. That's fifteen times five, or seventy-five new prospects. Now, if, of the seventy-five, sixty percent give you five referrals each . . . you get the picture. If you're out to build your client base exponentially (and why wouldn't you be?), you'll have trouble finding a better place to start than asking for referrals.

Referrals are the life blood of a successful career in sales. And yet salespeople are usually terrified to ask for them.

Often, they feel it will somehow threaten the relationship they've built up with a customer to ask if there are other associates of that customer who might benefit from their product or service. Perhaps the customer really doesn't like using the product or service after all, and asking for a referral will only intensify that feeling or bring it to the surface.

Conservatism is one thing. Paranoia is another.

Follow your instincts

You should be able to tell without too much difficulty whether or not you have a satisfied customer or an enthusiastic prospect. If you do, what that really means is that you have established the foundations of a productive, mutually beneficial relationship. Why on earth wouldn't your customer want to share that kind of relationship with his friends and associates? Assuming there is no competitive or other business conflict involved, there is every reason in the world to expect a referral—and one passed along happily and enthusiastically!

How can you make referrals work for you? Let's say your goal is to get five new prospects for the week. Carry with you at all times a package of 3" x 5" index cards. After you're done meeting with one of your customers or a good-quality prospect, simply say something like this.

"Mr. Jones, I'm willing to bet there are people in your (industry, area, related businesses) who could benefit from my talking to them about this (product/service)."

As you say this, you take out five index cards. Hold them in your hand. Let the prospect or customer see that there are five of them there. Then say, "Do you know of five people I could talk to?"

Help your contact along. It will be easier than you think; the fact that there are five separate index cards will make the task comprehensible and immediate. Your confident, professional attitude will guarantee that your request will not be seen as inappropriate.

Put the cards in a row on the desk as you fill them out, writing names only. Then, after you have identified the five referrals by name, go back and ask for the company affiliations, addresses, or other contact information. You do this because you want to make the first and most important job, identifying the people you can talk to, as easy as possible.

The direct approach

I know of one salesperson who will actually ask his contact at this point, "Frank, how would you feel about calling these people for me?" Of course, the contact says no and says the salesperson should make the call. Then the salesperson says, "Yeah, you're right, I probably should call them. You don't mind if I use your name, I hope?" He has never yet been turned down on the second question—which was the one he wanted a "yes" answer to in the first place.

That's an aggressive approach, and it's not one I'm sure I'd recommend to all salespeople. But it certainly illustrates the point that you can profit enormously when it comes to referrals by taking the initiative and asking for what you want!

Habit #13

Showing enthusiasm

No, this doesn't mean embracing your prospect, pumping hands twenty times as you shake, or issuing endless implausible compliments about dress or appearance.

There is a difference between enthusiasm and poorly disguised panic. Enthusiasm builds bridges. Panic tears them down.

A sales meeting is like any other interaction. It takes a certain amount of time to get off the ground. If you understand the dynamics that are at work when you first come into contact with a prospect, you will go a long way toward understanding how enthusiasm must be conveyed as the relationship progresses.

The early phase

When people meet someone new, they pass through a number of stages. There is among human beings a certain feeling-out process, an introductory stage. You cannot say convincingly at this stage all that you might want to about solving the prospect's problem, because the two of you don't know each other well enough yet. The prospect—along with most of the rest of the adult members of our species—will require a certain "choosing" time before entering into a socialization stage with another person. So the best way to show enthusiasm in the very early part of the meeting is to underplay it. Confident bearing; good eye contact (but not to such a degree it could be confused with staring); a firm handshake; predictable, smooth movements as you walk from one point to another—these are the keys to communicating your excitement about the new relationship you're trying to build.

The later phase

Only you can tell when the prospect enters the second stage of socialization, but rest assured that the change will be noticeable. It will be marked by a more relaxed, open approach, often reflected in less constricted body language. What you're looking for is the point at which the prospect listens not because he has agreed to do so, but because he wants to. Once you see that shift take place—and it may be during the first visit or during a subsequent one—you can change the "grammar" of your presentation.

You may decide to use your hands more in gesturing, or to use the prospect's preferred form of address ("Mr. Powers" or "Bill") somewhat more frequently. You might even feel comfortable using less formal phrasings and word choices: "Take a look for yourself." "How about that?" "And I'll tell you what we did."

Make an effort to avoid repetitive, mechanical gestures or responses. This is exactly what constitutes an unspontaneous, unenthusiastic meeting. If your conversational partner insisted on constantly nodding his head up and down, with little real regard for what you had to say, how would you feel?

Keep your eyes open

These are general guidelines; your individual interactions with prospects will vary, because prospects themselves will vary. The point is, bolstering your presentation with appropriate enthusiasm (especially on the second and subsequent visits) is an essential part of good salesmanship.

Habit #14

Giving yourself appropriate credit

Talk about yourself—but be humble.

The two instructions are not mutually exclusive. I want you to learn how to do both. There's nothing wrong with walking into the prospect's office and talking with confidence and pride about what you do. Too many salespeople can't seem to grasp that that's really the reason they show up in the first place! The only trap to watch out for is that of appearing arrogant. Fortunately, that's easy enough to avoid.

A balanced confidence

When you walk in to meet the prospect, you will want

to convey success, confidence, and flexibility. That's not arrogance. That's professionalism, and you should be proud of it. You should be able to talk, in detail, about the things that make you successful.

I am not suggesting you play one-up with your prospect by boasting about how great your kids look, how good your golf game is, or how much money you make. That's a game you can't win, no matter how the conversation ends.

What I'm suggesting is the aggressive promotion of your ability to succeed at your chosen task, and it requires a good deal of discretion on your part. You have to learn how to read the situation. You have to know when to step back. You have to know that what works for Prospect A in one situation may not work at all with Prospect B in another situation. What I'm suggesting carries the very real risk that, if you don't read the signals correctly, you may overwhelm your prospect. But it's still worth thinking about, because far too many salespeople underwhelm the prospect, and that's just as dangerous. At least with my way, you know there's no way you're going to fade into the anonymous parade of mediocre salespeople most decision-makers have to face!

Talk yourself up

Yes. There is a definite risk here. But in my view, it's a risk worth taking.

Try it with the next prospect you see.

"Mr. Jones, I am really glad to see you. This has

been a really big week for us—we just completed the XYZ project. Let me tell you about it."

Wow! Here's a person who makes things happen!

In an earlier chapter, we used a doctor/patient analogy. I'm going to revise it a little bit to make a different point here.

This time, suppose you walk into the doctor's office—and the minute the doctor walks in the door, you notice that he looks sicker than you do. He's wheezing and coughing—and holding a stubby, half-smoked cigarette between his fingers. He's tottering a little bit as he walks. His eyes are yellowish. He's having trouble focusing on things.

Is this the man who's going to solve your health problem?

For many professionals, there are two kinds of people: those who add value to whatever they touch, and those who cause the value of everything they touch to decline. Prove that you fall into that first category. Show your value! Demonstrate it! Broadcast it! Shout it from the rooftops! As long as you do so without affecting an air of superiority, your self-promotion will be perceived as security. Not arrogance, but admirable, enthusiastic, security in your own mission and your ability to carry it out.

Habit #15

Telling the truth
(it's easier to remember)

Someone did a study at a university recently on the issue of exactly how many "white lies" the average person tells during the course of a day. (Don't ask me how or why someone takes it into his head to study such a thing, or how he convinces someone else to pay for it.) Can you guess the results?

The answer came out to be approximately 200.

That's a lot of lying! And that's only the average. But let's be clear about what the researchers were looking for. When they went out looking for "white lies," they were looking for all the times someone said to someone else, "I'm glad you could come by today," when in fact maybe the person wasn't so glad. Those kinds of falsehoods—which we could also classify as harmless social convention—aren't what I'm talking about when I advise you to tell the truth to your client.

Building bridges

Salespeople are relationship-oriented. They build relationships on trust and personal contact, and they live and die on the strength of those relationships. Now, that this is the case serves as a convincing argument for telling the occasional "white social lie"—and against telling any other kind of lie. Let's look at a couple of examples.

"Gee, this is really a great office. I sure wish I worked in a place like this." (Actually, the office you work in easily outshines the prospect's.)

No big deal. Some salespeople find it easier to make a contact with the prospect by finding something like this to comment on as they're breaking the ice. What's the problem if there's a slight exaggeration on a point like this? Even if the prospect should somehow learn the terrible truth that you work in a spectacular office, is there any real downside to such a statement made tactfully, and without any overbearing flourishes? No.

"And about the delivery time you're asking for. I don't think we should have any problem meeting that, though I will have to clear it with the technical people after we square away the paperwork here today." (Actually, you know full well that you will miss the prospect's requested date by two weeks no matter what you say to the people in production.)

Red light! You are attempting to build a new relationship with a potential customer by deliberately misrepresenting your ability to solve his problem to his satisfaction. When things go crazy later on—and nine times out of ten in this situation, they will—the prospect is not going to remember the cute little disclaimer you slid in there about running things by the technical people. He's going to remember that you said you could deliver the product on the first, and the blankety-blank thing didn't make it into the warehouse until the fifteenth. At that stage, you will no longer be regarded as a problem-solver. You will be regarded as a problem: a salesperson who promises more than can be delivered. This is not the stuff of which repeat sales are made.

The slippery slope

If you need further convincing, consider this. Once you make a habit of simply telling everyone what they want to hear, you're eventually going to run into a serious problem: you won't be able to keep your story straight. You'll be dealing with fifteen different clients, each of whom has received fifteen different, customized pie-in-the-sky assurances. It will only be a matter of time until you become hopelessly muddled . . . and slip up disastrously.

Don't risk it. Tell the truth; it's easier to remember.

Habit #16

Selling yourself on yourself

Following are some ideas you can use to motivate yourself. Use them!

Don't listen to the radio during your morning commute

Radio broadcasts are usually filled with lots of depressing news that you won't be able to do anything about anyway. You'll hear soon enough about any news of consequence; take the morning for yourself. Buy some motivational tapes and make a habit of making the drive (or ride) in to work a time for positive messages and clearheaded, sober assessments of the day ahead. I know of one salesperson so committed to this principle that he honestly does not know whether or not the AM/FM radio in his car works!

Be specific with your goals—and your rewards

Perhaps your dream is to own a Lamborghini. Fine. Put a photo of one on your desk or on your refrigerator at home. Or perhaps you look at things a bit more analytically: your goal is to close six new sales over the next month. Take a piece of paper and commit the goal in writing. This will make your aims more tangible and increase the likelihood that they will be attained.

Get positive reinforcement

I think it's fascinating how many successful sales "teams" there are—two individuals who sell completely independently, but who rely on each other for constant support, advice, and constructive criticism. For most of us, this really is a far better alternative than going it alone; if you can establish such a relationship in your current work environment, give it a try and see what happens.

Get outside

Yes, you do need a lunch break. No, you shouldn't work through the noon hour. (My studies on this with salespeople lead me to believe that those who make a point of putting work aside for an hour and getting outside in the sunshine are actually more productive in terms of sales volume than those eager beavers who don't know when to quit.)

Leave yourself notes

"I can do it." "Most of the things I worry about never happen." "I have solved the problems of over 500 customers." Try to leave one on your desk Friday afternoon; you'll probably forget about it until Monday morning, when it will be a pleasant surprise.

Keep things in perspective

At my office, we make a habit of issuing a humorous reminder to each other: "It's not brain surgery." It isn't! Missed calls, forgotten deadlines, problems with customers . . . challenging as it all can be, it really isn't the end of the world. Sometimes things seem larger than they are. Try to keep that in mind as the day progresses. (For me, this lesson is particularly important between about two and four in the afternoon; that's when the day really can start to seem like an unending series of brain surgery projects. Is there a similar time for you? If so, that's when you should be sure to give yourself a break!)

Habit #17

Starting early

Did you know that you can often get past the "secretary trap" by making your important cold calls before 9:00 A.M.?

A lot of decision makers are given to making it into the office before the rest of the crowd shows up. They might just pick up their own phone if you call them then.

More benefits to an early start

That's one obvious advantage to getting an early start on the day. There are any number of others. For one thing, you'll be in a much better position to handle the office-wide crisis mentality that seems to set in around 9:01. For another, you'll be able to do your relaxing, newspaper-shuffling, and paperwork-managing at some time other than the peak contact hours during the business day. Those are advantages that can add up in a hurry. As I'm fond of pointing out, a salesperson is a lot like a retail store in that location is often the key requirement for success—only our location is the number of people you talk to during the day.

Commuting

There's more. My guess is that you'll find your commute a great deal easier if you get a little earlier start in the morning. That may seem like a minor consideration—until you realize how important attitude is in sales work. In so many of our big cities these days, you can spend an hour or an hour and a half simply getting from point A to point B in the morning. That's a lot of time, but the key consideration is really the aggravation you're likely to run into during that much "drive time" (or train or bus time, for that matter).

If you spend the first ninety minutes of every morning swearing at people or scowling at stop lights that seem designed to slow you down, you will probably find that your first few calls of the day are less than stellar. You'll lose the hop on your fastball before you talk to even a single potential customer—and that's a shame.

Time for yourself means making sure you're at your best when dealing with others

Finally, let me add an important observation, based on my experiences and those of many of the successful salespeople I've worked with: The day really does seem to go better if you take a couple of moments of "quiet time" for yourself before charging into the fray. There's something very hard on the system about bursting through the door at 8:59 and having to hit the ground running, no matter what that entails.

I have a strong feeling that salespeople who do this are costing themselves sales; the first few calls they make in the morning are "warmups," whether they like it or not. (Of course, the best of all possible worlds would be to show up for work early enough to have a little time for oneself, and then do some role-playing with a colleague to make sure the "warmup" calls aren't directed at live prospects.)

Habit #18

Reading industry publications (yours and your clients')

Quick! What kind of people do you suppose read *American Highway Engineer*?

How about *Publishers Weekly*? What audience do you expect would subscribe to *Adweek*? Or to *Billboard*? Or to *Variety*?

You may not find them on a lot of newsstands, but these publications, and hundreds more like them, may be the most important magazines you can get your hands on. The industry or industries you work in almost certainly have some sort of trade journal or magazine read by just about anyone of any consequence within the field. You can put yourself at a distinct competitive advantage in comparison with many salespeople by becoming familiar with these publications. Use them to keep abreast of industry trends. You should understand and be able to adapt to the business environment faced by your customers.

Subscriptions tend to be expensive, but you can probably find back issues of the magazine or journal you're looking for in any good big-city library.

Your winning edge: information

You will probably find that you can get much better understanding of the technical jargon employed in your target group by reading the articles in trade and professional magazines. Of course, you may have some trouble with a few of the denser articles aimed at subgroups within an industry, but you're much better off puzzling things through on paper now than nodding your head vacantly when the terms are rattled off later!

The "who's who" or "on the move" sections of these publications can be a particularly fertile source of sales leads. In these columns, you will find the names and company affiliations of people who have recently been promoted or hired at a given company. Who wouldn't be flattered by a brief note of congratulations on having appeared in such a column—followed up by a phone call a few days later to talk about your company's product or service?

Keeping track of it all

You might even decide to keep a running clip file on references to the various companies or individuals appearing in trade magazines. This can be an invaluable aid in breaking the ice when meeting with a new prospect. For my part, I can tell you right now that I'd much prefer being able to cite three interesting points about a prospect culled from the pages of a trade magazine than be forced to talk for twenty minutes about the weather or how attractive the prospect's kids are!

Habit #19

Supporting your visit the next day

Call or write your prospect the day after your visit. The vast majority of salespeople who mean to do this never actually get around to it. I strongly suggest that you build these contacts into your daily schedule or tickler system . . . so you can be absolutely certain to follow up during that crucial period after the meeting.

Don't try to initiate contact any later than one day after the visit with the prospect; the whole point of this "supporting" maneuver is to re-establish your presence and your commitment to solving the prospect's problems. Do so tactfully and without being overbearing.

25SALES HABITS OF HIGHLY SUCCESSFUL SALESPEOPLE

What it might sound like
in a telephone call

"Mr. Smith, this is Maude Powers at InfoWorld, Inc. I wanted to take a minute to thank you for taking time out of your schedule to meet with me yesterday. You know, I thought that meeting went really well yesterday. What did you think?"

I mention the phone contact first because it seems to be the most likely means of communication for such a message in today's sales environment. I should point out, though, that an old-fashioned typed or printed letter on company stationery can win a good deal of positive attention. It's less likely to happen, of course, because time is at such a premium these days (and because so many salespeople honestly don't care to write letters). But that can work to your favor: your courteous, neat, well-written letter will stand alone.

Don't rattle on and on in this piece of correspondence. The letter you send should be very brief!

The letter

Take a look at the following model; your letter should resemble it fairly closely.

April 24, 1992

Dear Mr. Smith:

I just wanted to drop a line to thank you for taking time out of your busy schedule to meet with me yesterday.

I found the ideas we exchanged very exciting, and I think you'll agree that there is the potential for a mutually beneficial relationship between your firm and ours. Mr. Smith, I hope you will feel free to call me if there are any questions or problems I can help you resolve.

Sincerely,

{written signature}

Maude Powers

Try it. What you'll find is that contacting the prospect in this way is an excellent way to win involvement and interest—and to reassert your credentials as a problem solver.

Warning: You can undo a lot of your hard work if you succumb to the temptation to try to close the sale during your "support" contact with the prospect. Keep to your cycle; use the call or letter to reinforce the points you felt were strongest about the meeting. Don't pressure the prospect or change the ground rules that have been established.

Habit #20

Giving speeches to business and civic groups

Public speaking rates as one of the most commonly shared fears human beings have. Yet I'm going to suggest that you take the time to develop your skills as a speaker and get out and share your (unparalleled!) expertise in your field with audiences—and not just audiences of people in your industry. Just about any audience, believe it or not, will do the trick.

The expert speaks

There is a double-edged sword at work here. First off,

you will benefit tremendously from the boost in confidence you receive from being treated as an expert in your field. By the way, if you don't consider yourself an expert in your field, you shouldn't be selling in it. Your customers are certainly counting on your expertise!

Think about it. You know your subject. You talk about it all day long. Once you can make the minor adjustment of being able to give a lecture about what you do, you'll be a lecturer. Get someone to note you, and you'll be a "noted lecturer." Pretty soon, there may well be a lot people noting you. Then you'll be a "widely noted lecturer." And deservedly so!

So the first benefit is reinforcement. You may know intellectually that you and your firm possess everything necessary to solve problems A, B, and C, but, believe me, you will receive an extraordinary emotional charge from actually getting up on stage and talking about A, B, and C to a group of willing listeners. If you don't think that that affirmation will carry over positively into the way you deal with prospects, my guess is you haven't been in sales very long.

The second benefit is even more remarkable. Studies have shown that when salespeople and consultants give speeches, an average of one out of every ten audience members will seek out the speaker afterwards to ask about his or her services. What this really means is that 10 percent of any given audience you talk to will end up qualifying itself—and entering your prospect cycle! Who knows what might happen if you actually took the initiative to shake some hands and pass out business cards during intermissions and at the event's conclusion?

It may take some effort on your part to get to the point where you feel comfortable addressing a group, but I assure you the effort will be worth it. Remember that even the most accomplished professional speakers complain of stage fright. Your goal should not be to get every butterfly out of your stomach, but to learn to make the adrenaline work for you.

Where to go to give the speech? Well, outside of the channels that may exist in your industry (such as addressing a trade conference or taking part in an annual convention), consider contacting your Chamber of Commerce about local round tables. Other possibilities include your area's Rotary Club, Kiwanis Club, or any group that seems relevant to the economy of your community or tied in somehow to what you do.

Go for it!

Go to the club or organization you've targeted, state your case, and see what happens. More often than not, they'll be glad to work you into the schedule.

So, ask yourself: What have I got to lose? Absolutely nothing! If it doesn't work out, at least you've made an effort—and gotten your name out in front of that many potential prospects. Give public speaking a try. Believe me, more than one salesperson has benefited tremendously from taking this route!

Habit #21

Passing along opportunity when appropriate

"What goes around, comes around."

This is a hard adage for a lot of salespeople to relate to, but it is nevertheless a vitally important point.

Lending a hand

Maintaining a can-do attitude where your own efforts are concerned is easy enough. But why on earth should you make an effort to help someone else out, if you don't have to—if there seems to be no logical way for that person to help you out somewhere down the line in your career?

The answer is complicated. Perhaps the best illustration I can give is to offer an example from the world of baseball.

Have you ever noticed that, after a baseball player hits a single, he will often joke around a little bit with the first baseman on the opposing team? That's a little odd, isn't it? Considering that these are top-echelon professional competitors dealing with members of the opposition, you'd expect a more stern, uncompromising mindset. But there they are joking, nodding, smiling at one another.

You usually can't hear what they're saying. Interestingly enough, it turns out that, both on the basepaths and in their other contacts, opposing players often discuss some aspect of the game they play for a living. Of course, they're not giving away important strategy points that would give any competitive advantage in the game at hand. But they are often discussing points of interest that concern their own development as ballplayers. Even though they may be on opposite teams, two shortstops, for instance, will often discuss the irregularities of the surface in a given park, or pass along information on how to play a member of a third team in another city who is managing to scoot a few too many hits through the infield lately.

They pass along these facts not because they do not see each other as competitors (they do!), but because they also see each other as colleagues—and it's not a bad idea to be known as the type of person who likes to help out a colleague. You might get your own hot tip on how to play that new guy who's tearing up the league! You don't know you're going to get such a tip, but because you're "part of the grapevine," you'll certainly get whatever is circulating.

Let me note here before I'm inundated with mail from baseball people about this that I'm talking about general trends among most ballplayers. You do find the occasional hard-nosed type who refuses to share a kind word with an opposing player, but that's the exception, not the rule. Many of these tight-lipped players are rookies whose main focus is on learning the ropes and remaining in the major leagues, and not on contributing to "the book"—which is what baseball players call the collection of accepted, widely circulated strategies currently influencing decisions among all teams.

Adding to "the book"

Is there a "book" in your league? If so, do you contribute to it? Do you share insights, leads, and contacts with others where appropriate, even though you cannot see any immediate benefit in doing so? There are hundreds, probably thousands of stories of strange, off-the-wall referrals generated "through the grapevine" that resulted in sales. To get your share, you'll need to develop a reputation as a person who contributes to that common pool of resources, tips, and openings.

Pass along opportunity when you can. It's a wise investment—one I've never heard any salesperson regret making.

Habit #22

Taking responsibility for presentations that go haywire

Assuming personal responsibility for the sale is a remarkably effective sales tool. It works so well that, if you're like me, the first time you hear about the technique, you'll probably wonder why on earth you didn't incorporate it into your sales routine long ago.

To start with, you have to be utterly, completely convinced in our own heart that you can offer your prospect the best possible solution to his problem. If that confidence isn't there, the technique I'm about to describe simply won't work. If the prospect (or anyone else) asks you to talk about your firm, you have to be able to reply with sincerity that you work for a one-of-a-kind, customer-first company and are proud to do so.

When you're on a sales visit, and you come to the closing stage, you simply ask the prospect when the best time would be for the product to be delivered or the service to start. One of two things will happen. Either the prospect will answer your question receptively—and thereby become a customer—or the prospect will back off and say no. If you find yourself facing the second scenario, you take responsibility.

Surprise!

At this point, the salespeople I know of who use this technique are genuinely taken aback—even shocked. And it's no act. They believe in their company so completely, and know so much about the prospect by this stage of the game, that they are legitimately concerned to see any evidence of a negative response to the proposal they've made. And they state that concern in no uncertain terms. You can too.

Here's what you say: "Mr. Jones, I'm really not sure what to say. I am so convinced that we have the best service, the best pricing, the best customization, and the best reputation of any firm in our industry that I can think of only one reason for you not to sign on with us. And that's that I must have done something terribly wrong just now in giving my presentation. So I'm going to ask you to give me a hand, Mr. Jones, and tell me where I went off course. Because, to be quite frank with you, sir, I know this service is right for you, and I'd really hate to have made a mistake like that."

What do you think you'll hear in response? One thing's for sure. It's not going to be easy for the prospect to come back with a run-of-the-mill brushoff like, "It's just not up our alley, Maureen." No, if you're Mr. Jones, you probably respect the person who had the courage to say that to you, who believes so strongly in the service you're looking at. You're going to pass along information—information on exactly what the problem is with your firm's signing on.

The common response you'll hear after you take responsibility for the initial "no" will sound something like this: "No, no, no, Maureen, it has nothing to do with you. It's on our end." And the prospect can then be expected to go into detail about the remaining obstacles. Then you have the facts you need to continue through the cycle.

Be sure you can deliver!

Let me repeat: This can be a startlingly effective technique, but it requires absolute faith on your part that you can in fact deliver on your promises. There is another catch, as well: you have to be willing to put aside the common fixation with "being right" we all share to a degree.

But when it comes right down to it, would you rather be "right"—or close a sale?

Habit #23

Being honest with yourself about the nature of the firm you work for

In my speeches and seminars, I often equate business with war, noting that each field of endeavor demands sound planning, has winners and losers, requires ammunition, features a chain of command, and so on. And I always conclude my remarks in this area by pointing out that business does have a few major advantages over war: nobody gets killed, and you can change armies.

Look at your job and yourself

Changing armies and the honest self-assessment that is often required to do so are the issues at hand. If you're currently in a work environment that does not meet your personal standards for quality, ethics, or orientation toward the customer, you should consider moving on. Too often, salespeople will stay with an "army" that's all wrong for them. The reasons given can be endless—don't have time, don't have the contacts, it's not really that bad here, lack of visibility in the industry—but, in the final analysis, they are all rationalizations, and unconvincing ones at that.

There is a danger here, because sometimes salespeople, who are a persuasive lot, will often go to great lengths to sell themselves on an idea. If that idea doesn't really work, the possibility of denial and self-deception looms. You may have to be on your guard, and make a special effort to be brutally honest with yourself about the direction both you and your firm are headed in.

Why? Because it's your career on the line. You want to work towards developing productive, mutually beneficial relationships with all the people you encounter on a professional level. If you find that your sales work now is not doing that for you—if you find that, to the contrary, you are leaving a trail of angry former customers in your wake—you are asking for trouble.

Games

Some salespeople try to play games with themselves. They try to rationalize a situation that is inherently manipulative or abusive, and see it as something it isn't and will never be. Don't be one of them. Don't set yourself up for a fall.

You have to feel it in your gut; you have to believe in your cause. You have to know in the marrow of your bones that all of your efforts are in line with your value system, and that that system encourages only productive, straight-shooter interactions. However you identify your goals, you must be certain that it is right for you to pursue them. You must know instinctively the benefit people will derive from working with you, and you must believe in your heart that all your company's efforts are for the best.

Otherwise you may well find that you have some difficulty succeeding.

Habit #24

Telling everyone you meet who you work for and what you sell

Why not?

Why not tell your doctor? Your electrician? Your dentist? The cab driver you rode with this morning? Your friend at another company? The person you sit next to on the airplane? Your barber? Members of the community group or charitable organization you work with? The guy who has the seat next to you at the ballgame?

Why not make a point of broadcasting your profession to anyone and everyone—with pride? I'm not suggesting you subject everyone you know to a sales pitch, of course. What I am suggesting is that it become second nature for you to say, loud and clear, to every single person you meet, bar none, that you're a salesperson for XYZ Corporation, maker of the finest widgets west of the Pecos. Couple that with a handshake and a confident, look-you-in-the-eye smile, and you know what? Every once in a while, someone's going to say, "Widgets, huh? You know, we've been thinking about those . . . ."

The secret

In my opinion, far too many salespeople have a pathological aversion to letting people know what they do for a living. The only reason I can come up with for this is that we often aren't quite as proud of what we do for a living as a brain surgeon might be, or an attorney, or an editor, or a scientist, or a teacher, or workers in any of dozens of categories who have no difficulty mentioning how they spend the majority of their waking hours.

We should be proud of being salespeople; I know I am! I know that the economy of the society I live in would not function without people who do what I do for a living, and I know that every transaction I undertake benefits all who are affected by it. Am I proud of that? You bet!

You should feel that way about your job, too. If you need to make some changes before you can feel that way, make the changes. Then look people in the eye and tell them what you do and who you do it for. Make it a habit; it may take a little work at first, but eventually you will begin passing along your name, profession, and company affiliation almost without thinking. (Here's a helpful hint: Current research indicates that a routine you stick with for twenty-one days will become in-grained, and will become a permanent habit you can incorporate automatically.)

Give it a try!

If you have to, start small and work your way up. You might begin by choosing friends or contacts you know well enough to talk to, but who don't yet know what you do for a living. But the easiest route by far is to say what you do for a living and who you do it for as you are introduced to someone. It's easier than you think, and it can pay tremendous dividends.

Habit #25

Keeping your sense of humor

Let's be honest. It can be tough to be a salesperson sometimes. Paradoxically enough, that's exactly why sales work has to be funny now and then.

I can only pass along my own observations about the salespeople I've worked with: Laughing helps. And not just around the edges. Laughing helps a lot. Salespeople depend on a good self-image more than any other professionals I know of, and it's awfully hard to keep a good self-image if you take yourself so seriously that you can't back off and laugh about the world once in a while.

Let me backtrack for a moment. One of the most scathing arguments against becoming a salesperson I know of is a very depressing film I saw some years back called *Salesman*. It's a documentary shot in grainy black-and-white about three traveling salespeople. It portrays sales as manipulative, demeaning, dishonest work—work that no thinking, feeling person would ever undertake voluntarily.

I have a real problem with that movie, for a couple of reasons. The first is that a great many people who aren't salespeople have been exposed to it, and have formed unrealistic stereotypes about my profession as a result. The second is that most of us who are salespeople haven't been exposed to it, and haven't been able to see the debilitating results of consistently bad sales work. This movie is convincing proof of how dangerous a salesperson with the wrong attitude can be, both to customers and to the salesperson himself. If you're a salesperson—and especially a salesperson who takes work very, very seriously—that movie will probably have a remarkable effect on you once you see it.

Mistakes

The salespeople in this film make just about every mistake in the book, including, but not limited to, failing to establish customer needs, lying to prospects, not listening to prospects, carrying a negative mental attitude, and failing to commit to their own ongoing professional development. But there's another error they make that, if it were rectified, could make all the other problems manageable.

They take the damned job too seriously and never give themselves a chance to decompress. It's difficult to attend to those other (admittedly catastrophic) problems if they've become part of your sales environment, but I can guarantee you here and now that there is no way on earth to approach your sales work the way it should be approached if you can't step back and laugh at yourself once in a while, preferably while on the job.

You matter!

You are too important a tool to yourself to run down. Take a break. Accept that it really is all right for you to miss the mark once in a while. Remember that you have to take the long view, and that today's catastrophe usually doesn't mean much tomorrow. This is a message that really never got to sink in as far as the salespeople in this movie were concerned. And they paid for it.

Don't let the World At Large talk you into thinking you're not in charge of your day, your month, your career. After all, you're the one with the answers; you're the professional solver of problems; you're the one who stays in control by keeping your head, asking the right questions, and being precise when it comes to giving necessary advice.

Lighten up and win! And remember: success couldn't happen to a nicer person.

Quick Reference Summary

Habit #1
Communicating the message that it is sound business to trust you

Don't cut corners at the expense of your own credibility—it's one of your most powerful weapons. Develop leadership skills. Build mutually beneficial long-term partnerships.

Habit #2
Asking the right questions

Ease in with simple questions that get the prospect talking about himself, then move on to the Past, the Present, and the Future—complementing each with Why and How. Use "middle-ground" questions when appropriate, but beware of overreliance on them. You must take responsibility for keeping the cycle moving forward.

Habit #3
Taking the lead

Tell the prospect where you are at any given point in the sales cycle. Don't be afraid to steer the conversation in the direction you want it to go. If there are questions or problems, you'll hear about them—and that's what you want! When in doubt, take the initiative in a calm, professional manner.

Habit #4
Engaging the prospect

Don't play ping-pong—work from the unique set of verbal and nonverbal cues your prospect will supply. Discuss that with which you are comfortable and familiar. Discuss the surroundings. "Lean in" when the prospect begins to talk about himself. Show care by really caring.

Habit #5
Finding key requirements

"Find a need and fill it" has its limits. For most of us, the day of relying exclusively or primarily on first-time customers has passed. Find requirements you can fill among those sought-after, qualified buyers who know full well that the choice is theirs.

Habit #6
Converting the leads that "fall into your lap"

The Sale You Deserve? Maybe. But take the time to establish a relationship and find out what's going on. Then ask to set up an in-person appointment. Don't assume you've got a "sure thing!"

Habit #7
Knowing how to make your product or service fit somewhere else

Does what you sell work in only one way? Or can you adjust it, make it serve some new purpose or function? Can you present it in a different light, or to a different group of people?

Habit #8
Pretending you're a consultant (because you are)

Don't improvise. If you need to take time out to come up with a workable solution, do so. Solving problems is the name of the game—and you have to listen before you can come up with a solution.

Habit #9
Asking for the next appointment while you're on the first visit

Perhaps the simplest, easiest-to-follow piece of advice in this book. Don't make excuses—make appointments!

Habit #10
Taking notes

Taking notes during your meeting with the prospect helps you listen, puts you in a position of authority, encourages your prospect to open up, and sends positive signals.

Habit #11
Creating a plan with each new prospect

It may be routine to you, but the prospect has never gone through the sales cycle with you before. Produce a customized, written plan based on your notes from early meetings. Remember, you're the doctor—don't rush the diagnosis!

Habit #12
Asking for referrals

Don't be shy—you can't afford it. Referrals are the life blood of a successful career in sales. Carry a package of three-by-five cards with you at all times; say, "I'm willing to bet there are people in your (industry, area, related business) who could benefit from my talking to them about this (product/service). Do you know of five people I could talk to?"

Habit #13
Showing enthusiasm

Talk up your company—and remember that there is a difference between enthusiasm and poorly disguised panic. Enthusiasm builds bridges; panic tears them down.

Habit #14
Giving yourself appropriate credit

Talk about yourself—but be humble. (No, the two aren't mutually exclusive. Convey success, confidence, and flexibility. Highlight past successes, but don't try to one-up the prospect. Try to exhibit the characteristics of a person who makes things happen.

Habit #15
Telling the truth (it's easier to remember)

We tell, on average, 200 lies every day! Well, social conventions and pleasantries are one thing—misleading the prospect about your ability to meet a deadline or deliver quality is quite another. Remember, your credibility is a precious asset. Defend it!

Habit #16
Selling yourself on yourself

Motivate yourself! Avoid the radio during your morning commute; listen to motivational tapes instead. Be specific with your goals—and your rewards. Get positive reinforcement. Get outside. Leave yourself notes. Keep things in perspective.

Habit #17
Starting early

There is a world before 9:00 A.M.! You can beat the secretary trap, ease your commute, reduce your aggravation, and improve your attitude by making it in an hour or so before everyone else does. It may sound tough—try it anyway. You'll be a convert before you know it.

Habit #18
Reading industry publications (yours and your clients')

Trade journals and newsletters are invaluable data sources; read them. These publications are fertile sources of leads, industry gossip, and all manner of important inside stuff. Take advantage of them!

Habit #19
Supporting your visit the next day

Call or write your present prospect the day after your visit. The vast majority of people who mean to do this never actually get around to it. Build this step into your schedule!

Habit #20
Giving speeches to business and civic groups

You will benefit tremendously from the boost in confidence you receive from being treated as an expert in your field (which you are); in addition, an average of one out of every ten audience members will seek you out to ask about your services.

Habit #21
Passing along opportunity when appropriate

"What goes around, comes around." Being a part of the "grapevine" is a wise decision—one I've never heard any salesperson regret making.

Habit #22
Taking responsibility for presentations that go haywire

Rejected? Try this: "Mr. Jones, I just don't understand . . . I must have made a mistake in my presentation for you to decide it this way. I know we can help you. Can you help *me* and show me where things went wrong?" You may have to put aside the common fixation with being "right"—but, then again, would you rather be "right" or close a sale?

Habit #23
Being honest with yourself about the nature of the firm you work for

If you have to choose between fighting a losing battle for losing generals and finding another army, find another army. Don't rationalize.

Habit #24
Telling everyone you meet who you work for and what you sell

Why not make a point of broadcasting your profession to anyone and everyone—with pride? This is not the same as subjecting everyone you meet to a sales pitch! Simply pass along your name, profession, and company affiliation to every new person you meet.

Habit #25
Keeping your sense of humor

It can be tough to be a salesperson sometimes—but that's why sales work has to be funny now and than! Lighten up—and remember, success couldn't happen to a nicer person.

Stephan Schiffman has trained over 250,000 salespeople at firms such as AT&T Information Systems, Chemical Bank, Manufacturers Hanover Trust, Motorola, and U.S. Healthcare. Mr. Schiffman, president of DEI Management Group, is the author of *Cold Calling Techniques (That Really Work!)*, *The 25 Most Common Sales Mistakes—and How to Avoid Them*, and a number of other popular books on sales.

Do you have questions, comments, or suggestions regarding this book? Please share them with me! Write to me at this address:

Stephan Schiffman
c/o Adams Media Corporation
57 Littlefield St.
Avon, MA 02322